tweetonomics

tweetonomics

Everything you need to
know about economics
in 140 characters or less

Nic Compton, Adam Fishwick, & Katie Huston

Illustrated by
Daniel Mackie

First edition for the United States, its territories
and dependencies, and Canada published in 2010
by Barron's Educational Series, Inc.

This book was conceived,
designed, and produced by
Ivy Press
210 High Street,
Lewes,
East Sussex, BN7 2NS, U.K.

All inquiries should be addressed to:
Barron's Educational Series, Inc.
250 Wireless Boulevard
Hauppauge, NY 11788
www.barronseduc.com

ISBN-13: 978-0-7641-4565-0
ISBN-10: 0-7641-4565-7

Library of Congress Control Number: 2010923344

Creative Director Peter Bridgewater
Publisher Jason Hook
Art Director Michael Whitehead
Editorial Director Caroline Earle
Senior Editor Lorraine Turner
Consultant Reader Dr. Elia Kacapyr
Design Ginny Zeal
Illustrator Daniel Mackie

Printed in India
Color Origination by Ivy Press Reprographics

9 8 7 6 5 4 3 2 1

Contents

Introduction

Airplane crashes make big headlines. So do train crashes. And so, it turns out, do financial crashes. The subprime mortgage crisis of 2007, and the near-collapse of the banking system that followed, inspired blanket coverage from the media. Never before had so many acres of newsprint been devoted to the arcane workings of the financial system; never before had so many hours of television been expended on scrutinizing the behavior of our gung-ho bankers.

One thing that soon became clear, though, was that not everyone was going to bother spelling out exactly what an "asset-backed security" was, or why it was important to the crisis; or how "credit default swaps" could bring down a company—and very nearly a whole financial system; or what "leverage" meant and how it could turn cautious men into crazed, out-of-control gamblers.

This book will present these sometimes complex ideas in a form easily digested by the nonexpert. And what could be easier to digest than the now-ubiquitous bite-sized "tweets?"

Trying to write about economics in 140 characters may seem like a silly idea. After all, entire books are devoted to subjects such as monetarism, so what could we hope to achieve in a few tweets? But there's no doubt that having to pare things down and cut words to a minimum can lead to a startling degree of clarity. Yes, some of the nuances might be lost, but the reward, when it works, is an immediate understanding of some quite complicated ideas. And that's surely something worth striving for.

Our starting point in this book are the terms used every day in the news, usually with insufficient explanation. Terms such as the "free market," "supply and demand," "fiscal and monetary policy." From there, we broaden out to some of the big ideas that have shaped our economies, such as Keynesianism, neo-liberalism, and Marxism, and meet some of the personalities involved (Keynes, Friedman, Hayek). An overview of the workings of stock markets takes us straight into boom and bust—and back to the 2007–09 crisis. We then look at how economic policies have had an impact on the global stage, before turning our attention to green economics to see whether this might offer any long-term solutions to financial malaise.

This book doesn't pretend to be a comprehensive textbook on economics, but it will be a useful companion to anyone listening to the news or reading the paper, especially in times of financial turmoil. And, if reading these tweets tempts you to find out more about aspects of economics than we have had space to write about here, then our mission will have been accomplished.

How the economy works

What makes the butcher, the brewer, and the baker get up in the morning to open the store and sell their wares? What are the key factors that decide whether they expand into a multimillion dollar business or simply close up shop and go home? These are the key principles of economics.

What is the free market?

A true free market is one where production of goods is controlled purely through supply and demand. No regulation. No subsidies. No taxes.

Government should only intervene to prevent coercion, fraud, and abuse of property rights. Minimal taxes should be raised for doing this.

This allows everyone to compete on an even playing field without artificial hindrance or support. And may the best man/woman win.

Supply and demand regulate the price and availability of goods far more efficiently than any amount of planning, especially by government.

The magic of supply vs. demand vs. price. It is what Adam Smith called the "invisible hand of the market."

He pointed out that the baker and the butcher sell bread and meat not out of kindness but to make a living, yet all of society benefits.

What are supply and demand?

Supply and demand are what drive a free market economy. Understand how they work and you're on your way to becoming an economist.

The law of the market says the higher the price of goods, the less the demand. That's because no one wants to pay more than they have to.

The same law states that the higher the price of goods, the greater the supply. That's because there's a better chance of making a profit.

The point at which supply matches demand is called equilibrium. This is optimal as nothing is wasted and everyone gets what they want.

But equilibrium is rarely reached, and prices are constantly responding to shifts in supply and demand. Just look at the price of computers.

Some products are said to be "elastic." That means people don't really need them, so a small change in price will drastically reduce sales.

"Nonelastic" products are things we consider essential or impossible to substitute (e.g., oil), and which we'll buy regardless of cost.

What is consumption?

Consumption is the amount of goods and services purchased by people. It usually makes up the biggest part of a country's GDP (see page 20).

Traditionally, economists tended to focus on the manufacture of goods and ignored consumption. John Maynard Keynes changed all that.

The main areas of consumption are: durables (housing, cars), nondurables (food, clothing), and services (health, transport, communication).

The proportion of income you spend on each is a good indication of your level of affluence—regardless of salary. It's your quality of life.

What is competition?

When two or more firms operate in the same market, supplying similar products, each trying to maximize their profits, you have competition.

Most economists believe that competition within a free market is the best way to ensure the distribution of affordable goods and services.

Competition encourages companies to develop new products and services to attract customers, and it forces them to keep their prices low.

Others believe that competition is inefficient, as companies duplicate processes to compete against one another in similar markets.

What is a monopoly/ oligopoly?

Where a firm dominates a market to the exclusion of all others, you have a monopoly. Where very few firms dominate, you have an oligopoly.

Companies with a monopoly tend to produce a smaller number of goods at a higher price.

This impoverishes society because fewer people enjoy the benefits of the product, and disproportionate profits go to well-off shareholders.

High start-up costs and economies of scale give an established company an advantage over a new company and safeguard its monopoly.

Companies in an oligopoly may form a cartel, officially or otherwise, and "fix" prices artificially high.

Some markets, such as water, are a "natural" monopoly. They are usually controlled by a government regulator, which sets prices.

What is regulation?

Regulation is usually implemented to correct a perceived failure in the market and achieve some economic, social, or environmental benefit.

In reality, no market is truly "free." Governments intervene all the time to control our behavior. Taxing fuel and cigarettes is an example.

Regulation is used to license manufacturers and service providers to guarantee minimum standards in areas such as food and construction.

It is also used to safeguard the rights of workers through safety standards and minimum wage, and to protect the environment.

And it is used to control natural monopolies, such as water and electricity, to ensure consumers pay a fair price and receive good service.

Free marketeers oppose the use of regulations in all areas of economic life—other than to protect life, liberty, and property.

They argue that regulation is a disincentive to business and usually has consequences other than those intended.

Many markets were deregulated in the 1980s, under Ronald Reagan in the U.S. and Margaret Thatcher in the U.K.

What is debt?

Debt is the borrowing of credit from banks and other institutions (multilateral borrowing), or from other countries (bilateral borrowing).

Governments can also borrow internally by issuing securities and government bonds, or by printing bank notes.

As of June 2009, the U.S. had the greatest foreign currency debt ($13.45 trillion), followed by the U.K. ($9 trillion).

The World Bank was formed to help developing countries, providing loans where private finance wasn't available, albeit at the market rate.

The 1970's oil crisis caused many developing countries to become more indebted and forced them to introduce unpopular austerity measures.

By 2002, Africa owed $295 billion. It's been estimated that for every $1 Africa receives in aid, it pays $3 back in debt repayment.

What is inflation?

Inflation is an increase in the overall cost of living, as measured by indices such as the CPI (Consumer Price Index).

Inflation is bad for business because it creates uncertainty and discourages investment. Also, as prices rise, workers demand higher wages.

Inflation is bad for savers and people on fixed incomes. But it's good for borrowers, as the cost of borrowing in "real" terms is reduced.

A low rate of inflation also encourages consumer spending and creates employment—as demonstrated by the Phillips Curve.

Most economists agree that inflation is the result of too much growth in the money supply—that is, the amount of money in the economy.

Most economists advocate reducing the amount of money in circulation, as well as increasing taxes and reining in government expenditure.

What is deflation?

Deflation, the opposite of inflation, is a reduction in the cost of living, as measured by indices such as the CSI (Consumer Spending Index).

It is caused by a reduction in money supply and diminished spending. This means the price of goods falls, but the value of money stays high.

As prices fall, consumers feel disinclined to spend, figuring that they may as well wait until prices drop further.

Deflation also means property is worth less in "real" terms, leading to a loss of confidence, and encouraging people to save more.

It's a vicious spiral: As production declines, workers are laid off, factories are closed, and people have even less money to spend.

The cure is often a mix of "quantitative easing," putting money back into the economy, and lowering interest rates to encourage spending.

Economists were baffled by the arrival of "stagflation" in the 1970s—a mix of stagnation and inflation that had been thought impossible.

What is capital?

In classical economics, capital is one of three "factors of production" in industry, the others being land and labor.

As well as financial assets, it includes buildings, tools, vehicles, and other items used in the process of production—but not raw materials.

In personal terms, capital includes your home, furniture, car, stocks—even that stamp collection you inherited is part of your capital.

If you make a profit selling a capital item, you are liable to pay capital gains tax.

Other types of capital are becoming increasingly important. These include natural capital, or the value of natural features, such as rivers.

"Social capital" refers to the social networks in an economy. "Intellectual capital" refers to the value of ideas.

 # What is human capital?

Human capital refers to the knowledge, skill, and personal attributes (such as punctuality, motivation, and honesty) of a workforce.

In classical economics, workers were usually regarded simply as "labor" that could be replaced at will. That all changed in the 1950-60s.

New research showed that investment in education, training, and health could bring enormous benefits to a country's economy.

This resource was described as human capital because it represented a permanent asset, not an expendable material.

Jacob Mincer and Gary Becker were pioneers of the new approach, which linked social causes with economic outcomes, and vice versa.

They identified "specific" and "general" capital: "specific" skills useful to particular employees and "general" abilities useful to all.

And they showed that an individual's personal upbringing can influence his/her competence in the workplace just as much as formal training.

 # What is a labor market?

In classical economics, labor works like any other market: supply and demand determine price (wage) and quantity (numbers employed).

In a perfectly free market, a point of equilibrium can be reached where supply matches demand and there is no unemployment.

By this theory, unemployment is caused by workers refusing to accept the "equilibrium wage." Most unemployment is therefore voluntary.

In fact, a high level of unemployment benefits employers because it provides a constant pool of labor and helps to keep wages low.

Keynes challenged the view that high unemployment is inevitable by advocating stimulus spending to increase employment opportunities.

The market view ignores the "human element," including the influence of personal connections in finding work, and geographical factors.

What is productivity?

Productivity is a measure of a company's (or country's) output compared to the number of hours worked by its employees.

In other words, productivity equals output divided by hours worked.

A company can improve productivity by increasing its output for the same number of worker hours, or by producing the same output quicker.

Productivity is often increased through developments in technology, thereby reducing the amount of time it takes to make a product.

Introduction of assembly lines and "time-motion" work practices in U.S. factories in the 1900s halved the time it took to build a car.

Increases in productivity can also be achieved through wage incentives and improvements in the work environment.

What is GDP?

GDP stands for Gross Domestic Product. It is the sum of all goods and services consumed in a country within a year.

GDP also includes investment, government spending, and net exports.

"Net exports" is the difference between how much a country imports and how much it exports. It's also known as the balance of trade.

GDP is a useful measure of the amount of economic activity in a country, but a poor measure of standard of living and/or quality of life.

GDP omits many important things. For example: the gap between rich and poor; economic longevity; and environmental sustainability.

The Human Development Index (HDI) attempts to measure quality of life. It combines GDP with factors such as life expectancy and education.

Other indices include the Genuine Progress Indicator, Gross National Happiness, European Quality of Life Survey, and Happy Planet Index.

As at 2009, the U.S. had the highest GDP at $14.26 trillion, compared to $14.5 trillion for the entire European Union.

What is the balance of trade?

The balance of trade is the difference between how much a country imports and how much it exports. It's also known as net exports.

A country that exports more than it imports has a trade surplus; a country that imports more than it exports has a trade deficit.

Traditionally, most countries try to export more than they import in order to stimulate the economy and build up foreign currency reserves.

Since the 1960s, the U.S. has run a trade deficit. To fund this it prints more dollars. As long as we all collect dollars, this is okay.

As of 2009, the U.S. trade deficit stood at $380 billion, compared to China's trade surplus of $296 billion.

What is credit?

Simply put, credit is borrowed money: You get something now—like money, goods, or services—by agreeing to pay for it later.

Credit is usually given by banks. When you use a credit card, take out a home mortgage, or get a loan to buy a car, you're buying on credit.

Credit is useful: It can help you buy things online or abroad, spread out costs of big buys, or allow you to start a small business.

When you buy on credit, you owe money, so you're in debt. And you owe more than you spent, thanks to interest—a fee for taking out credit.

If you don't pay back a debt, you default. No lender wants that, so banks use credit ratings and do credit checks before lending money.

What is a credit crunch?

A credit crunch is when credit is harder to obtain. Banks are less willing to lend money to people, businesses, and to each other.

It can happen when many people default on loans, when market prices fluctuate, or when the government makes new laws about lending.

It's also fueled by fear: If banks are scared that other banks have no money, they don't give any credit. It's a self-fulfilling prophecy.

In a credit crunch, banks make tougher rules for loans, so people whose credit was good enough before can no longer get a mortgage.

Credit costs more: Interest rates are high because banks want to cover their risk, so mortgages are expensive and credit card rates go up.

Stock markets also fall, because with less money and credit available, confidence drops. That's why investments and pensions are worth less.

When credit is more expensive and harder to come by, investment in business and consumer spending falls, too.

What caused the 2007 credit crunch?

Before the crunch, credit was very easy to get, and people took on credit that they couldn't pay back.

Banks in the U.S. gave mortgages to people who wouldn't usually qualify, called "subprime mortgages."

Banks made risky subprime loans because they had higher interest rates and opening fees, so it was a good way for banks to make money.

When house prices fell, many people couldn't pay their mortgages. Banks lost a lot of money, so they lent less and charged more for it.

The defaults didn't just affect one bank; they hit a complicated web of banks and companies, which turned it into a global credit crunch.

Banks sold subprime mortgages to other banks, agencies, and companies, such as Fannie Mae and Freddie Mac.

What is investment?

An investment is the purchase of equipment, skills, or technology in order to produce goods. It is a kind of gamble.

If the gamble pays off, productivity will improve and the company's profits will increase. If it fails, the investment may be lost (sunk).

It differs from capital, which relies on interest and/or appreciation of the asset to produce a return.

There is a thin line between investment and speculation. Investment may have long-term benefits; speculation is about making a fast buck.

Investment comes from the Latin word for clothing, "vestis," referring to putting something (i.e., money) in someone else's pocket.

High interest rates usually lead to low investment, as the return from improved productivity may not match the return from savings.

Low interest rates usually lead to high investment because it's cheaper to borrow money and gamble on an increase in productivity.

What is innovation?

Innovation is the development of a product through improvements in technology, knowledge, and/or marketing.

In a competitive market, innovation can have a greater impact on profitability than improving efficiency or competing on price alone.

Innovation drives most economic peaks: the Industrial Revolution in the 1800s, factories in the 1900s, and communications in the 2000s.

The economist Joseph Schumpeter highlighted the importance of innovation in the 1940s, saying companies should be more proactive about it.

 # What are property rights?

Property rights determine who owns a resource, who decides how it is used, and who profits from leasing or selling it.

Property rights are a key part of capitalism. Only by clearly defining who owns what can you motivate people to truck, barter, and trade.

The failure of communism is often linked to property rights. Without private ownership, no one was motivated to make enterprises profitable.

Eco-degradation is sometimes linked to property rights. If ownership of the environment was clearly assigned, it would be better protected.

Intellectual property rights include industrial (inventions, designs) and artistic (paintings, novels, music) property.

The World Trade Organization (WTO) has devised an Agreement on Trade-Related Aspects of Intellectual Property Rights (TRIPS).

TRIPS strengthens property rights and commits governments to ensuring copyrights are properly enforced in their territories.

Since the majority of patents are owned by the West, this puts developing countries at a big disadvantage. The gap is widening every year.

What governments do

Even in a so-called free market economy, markets aren't really completely free. Governments can't help meddling in order to influence the outcome—often with good reason. So what can governments do and what effect do their policies have on the economy? Are you a supply-sider or a demand-sider?

What are fiscal policies?

Fiscal policy is the fancy name given to government spending and taxation policies, and whether what's coming in matches what's going out.

In general, these policies are used by governments when they want to change overall demand or redistribute income within the economy.

They can be neutral, contractionary, or expansionary: keep a balanced budget, spend less to reduce deficits, or spend more to boost activity.

Contractionary policies require raising taxation or cutting budgets. Not only does it reduce deficits, but it can also rein in inflation.

Expansionary policies are the opposite. Often the aim is to reduce unemployment by lowering taxes or increasing government spending.

What are monetary policies?

Monetary policies deal with exactly what you would expect—they are policies that control the supply and cost of money.

Unlike fiscal policies, they tend to be made independently of central government—in most countries it is the central bank that decides.

Management of the money supply is seen as the most important way to prevent high inflation and ensure stable long-term growth.

Policies can be either contractionary or expansionary. But rather than managing budgets, the aim is to control inflation.

Contractionary policies aim to reduce inflation by limiting the money supply and reducing demand.

Expansionary policies aim to boost economic activity by doing the opposite, but at the risk of raising inflation.

But how do you control the cost? Simple. A rise in the central bank interest rate raises the cost of borrowing for banks, business, and you.

Milton Friedman famously advocated that governments prioritize monetary over fiscal policies. This position was known as "monetarism."

 # What are interest rates?

Interest rates are the price of borrowing, as well as the return you receive for keeping your money in the bank.

Loans must be repaid plus interest charges. If you "lend" your money to a bank by putting it in a savings account, you expect it to grow.

While commercial banks set their own competitive rates, central banks decide the rate from which these are determined—the discount rate.

This discount rate is basically another name for the interest rate and is set in line with policy priorities and the needs of the economy.

This is a vital policy tool—by raising or lowering interest rates, government can influence lending and spending throughout the economy.

The announced rate is called the nominal rate. More important is the "real" rate, which is simply the nominal rate adjusted for inflation.

What is a central bank?

With their wide array of functions and links to the government and market, central banks can be thought of as the brains of an economy.

Important examples of central banks are the U.S. Federal Reserve, the Bank of England, and the recently established European Central Bank.

Only they can print money. This prevents uncontrolled expansion of the money supply that influences everything from inflation to investment.

Not only do they control the money supply, they also provide loans to government and national banks, and, in some cases, enforce regulation.

The Fed describes its duties as "monetary policy ... supervising and regulating banking ... maintaining stability ... providing financial services."

A central bank is not to be confused with a national bank, which can be a wholly state-owned institution or a private commercial enterprise.

What is financial regulation?

Regulations stop banks from misbehaving. They cover the rules, restrictions, and guidelines that financial institutions must adhere to.

They are often independent agencies, like the U.S. Securities and Exchange Commission (SEC) or the U.K. Financial Services Authority (FSA).

The SEC says its "mission ... is to protect investors, maintain fair, orderly, and efficient markets, and facilitate capital formation."

Regulators emphasize the need to maintain a balance between regulating and allowing free markets, a balance that is often difficult.

Over the last few decades this balance has shifted toward deregulation, or re-regulation, which has created more relaxed financial markets.

This more relaxed environment has been blamed for the 2007 crisis that began in the financial sector and then spread to the real economy.

 # What is taxation?

Taxation is a way for governments to raise revenue from you, me, and the businesses operating within their territories.

Forms of taxation include income tax and Social Security payments for individuals, and state and federal corporate taxes for businesses.

Redistribution can also be achieved through taxation—progressive taxes either on luxury goods or higher incomes can produce this effect.

In the opposite direction, regressive taxation can produce redistribution too—by increasing the tax burden on lower-income individuals.

The phrase "no taxation without representation" was used to capture the grievances of the American independence movement.

This highlights the link between taxation and democracy—governments need revenue, but those taxed have a right to say how it is spent.

What is privatization?

Privatization occurs when government-owned assets, such as railways, airlines, or postal services, are transferred into private hands.

In the 1980s, Ronald Reagan in the U.S. and Margaret Thatcher in the U. K. pursued privatization policies.

Those who favor privatization claim that it reduces inefficiency by removing lumbering bureaucracy and the potential for corruption.

Supporters argue that government-owned firms slow economic growth by concentrating on the priorities of politicians rather than the market.

Opponents of privatization claim that it makes public services less accountable to those that use them—the public.

Privatization can also result in the transfer of government assets to political allies—corruption that is difficult to trace.

What are demand-side policies?

Demand-side policies are the tools used to affect the overall demand in an economy. They either increase or decrease our ability to spend.

Both monetary and fiscal policy can influence demand: Lowering interest rates can boost demand the same as increasing government spending.

Lower interest rates encourage businesses to borrow. They also lower the cost of mortgages or other debts for the public.

Government spending is an important demand-side tool—these policies are usually targeted at reducing unemployment.

Increased employment produces a virtuous circle of growth, as more jobs create more demand that then encourages more production.

But this often requires a difficult trade-off: If demand grows too fast for supply, there is a danger of triggering high inflation.

 # What are supply-side policies?

Supply-side policies increase the overall productivity of an economy. They provide incentives for individuals and businesses to work harder.

They are associated with policymakers opposed to strong government intervention in the economy—those who think less is more.

Deregulation and reducing tax and government spending are the most important supply-side tools—each targets specific areas of the economy.

Deregulation arguably increases competition between businesses as well as the flexibility of the marketplace.

Flexibility is associated mainly with the labor market—more competition means that individuals will be more productive in their jobs.

Reducing income tax and government spending on welfare is also claimed to encourage individuals to work harder.

Lower income taxes mean that there is more reward for higher paid (more productive) jobs, and less welfare makes not working more costly.

What were Reaganomics?

Reaganomics is the collective name given to supply-side economic policies of the Reagan administration during the 1980s.

Responding to inflation and stagnation, it sought to boost growth through smaller government and support for private enterprise.

In an attack on post-war Keynesianism, the main policy objectives were to reduce government spending, income tax, regulation, and inflation.

Reagan famously said: "Only by reducing the growth of government can we increase the growth of the economy."

Income tax rates were reduced under Reaganomics: The highest rate fell from 70 percent to 28 percent, but spending was not cut.

Increases in defense spending led to significant rises in U.S. public debt, and budget and trade deficits that still haven't gone away!

What is a public-private initiative?

A public-private initiative is a partnership between a government and private business that usually provides some sort of public service.

Roads, water, waste management, and prisons—in many cases these public services are now contracted out to private business.

Even the Defense Department is increasingly making use of the private sector by contracting out support services such as housing.

For the government, costs to the taxpayer can be reduced; much of the finance for the project must be raised by the private business.

For the business, government subsidies, tax breaks, and guaranteed revenues provide a strong incentive to enter into such an initiative.

Collaboration between the World Health Organization and the pharmaceutical industry shows the international significance of partnership.

 # What is a cap-and-trade scheme?

A cap-and-trade scheme is a mixed government and market-based approach to pollution reduction. You have to pay to pollute!

The Environmental Protection Agency describes it as "an environmental policy tool ... providing [polluters] flexibility in how they comply."

The largest of these schemes is the European Union Emissions Trading Scheme, which covers the emissions of over 10,000 installations.

The cap is a mandatory limit on polluting, usually set by a government agency that issues a set emission allowance to businesses.

The trade is the buying and selling of these allowances by those businesses that emit more or less than the set allowance.

By charging those who pollute more, this scheme arguably provides economic incentives that reduce pollution.

The big ideas

So what do all of these policies mean? What are the main schools of thought in economics? Depending on how you mix these ideas, you might be considered a liberal, a neo-liberal, a Keynesian, or even a Marxist. It pays to know which brand of economics you believe in.

What is liberalism?

Liberalism is an economic philosophy that states that the free market is the best way to organize the economy.

Liberals think the state should not intervene in the economy. They coined the phrase "the night-watchman state."

The state's only economic role is to ensure the market works freely and that private property is not violated.

The free market will deliver the best result because it allocates resources in the most efficient way.

This happens because of the law of supply and demand, which makes sure markets clear out—no surpluses or shortages in a free market.

If no one distorts the market and everyone knows everything that's going on, the market settles at equilibrium.

If something goes wrong, the market will solve the problem on its own. The government shouldn't intervene. It will only make things worse.

What is neo-liberalism?

Neo-liberalism is an economic philosophy inspired by liberalism. It refers to the policies that replaced Keynesianism after the 1970s.

Neo-liberals think the most important thing a government should get right is to keep low inflation, not full employment.

Like liberals, neo-liberals think the state shouldn't intervene in the economy. It always makes a mess of it.

That's why neo-liberals believe that central banks like the Federal Reserve should be independent from the government.

You don't want politicians telling central bankers to lower interest rates so that unemployment doesn't go up.

And unemployment? Well, it's the unions' fault because they distort the labor market; otherwise it would regulate itself as it always does.

If you try to reduce unemployment by cutting interest rates, you get inflation—and that's the last thing you need.

The three things a neo-liberal loves most are privatization, deregulation, and flexibility of the labor market.

 # What is monetarism?

Monetarism, as the name suggests, is an approach that focuses on monetary policy. Controlling the money supply is vital to a stable economy.

The amount of money in an economy affects short-term consumption, business, and people's investment decisions— more money equals more activity.

The real innovation of this idea is in the long term—by concentrating on effective monetary policy, governments can keep prices stable.

By keeping prices stable, the economy will not experience any high rates of inflation, and output and consumption will grow at a steady rate.

Controlled and constant increase of the money supply will keep inflation low while expanding economic activity.

Monetarists argue that these long-term benefits are better than any short-term gains that come from targeting demand over supply.

What is comparative advantage?

Despite being first formulated in 1817, comparative advantage remains one of the most influential theories of international trade.

According to this theory, gains from trade are to be calculated not from any absolute advantage a country may have.

Instead, comparative advantage is what is important. This means we need to consider the relative prices of production within a country.

Even if the U.S. can produce both cars and computers cheaper than France, choosing to produce the relatively cheaper option is best.

If the U.S. produces excess computers and trades them for French cars, overall output and consumption would be increased.

By each country specializing and pursuing comparative advantage, all can experience gains from international trade.

What is redistribution?

Redistribution is when the government intervenes in the economy to shift income from one group of people to another.

Most people believe that redistribution benefits the poor rather than the rich—a kind of modern Robin Hood.

That's why it's associated with progressive taxation—taxing the rich to give to the poor.

The best example is income tax. Rich people pay higher taxes and this money is paid out to poor people in the form of welfare benefits.

Corporation tax is another example of redistribution. The government taxes corporate profits in order to fund welfare programs.

Supporters of redistribution say it makes the system less unjust—you need to reform capitalism.

 # What is social democracy?

Social democracy is a political and economic ideology that provides a middle ground between socialism and free-market capitalism.

The aims of social democracy are to improve capitalism to make it fairer and more equitable—reform, not revolution!

In economic terms, it is associated with the emergence of the welfare state across Europe, and welfare programs in the U.S.

Unlike socialism, private ownership of production remains unchallenged in a social democratic system. Regulation and labor rights are the priority.

Progressive taxation—taking from the rich to give to the poor—provides the main source of government revenue to boost public welfare.

Critics on the right claim that social democracy gives too much power to the state. Critics on the left argue reform doesn't go far enough.

What is Keynesianism?

Keynesianism is an economic theory based on the ideas of John Maynard Keynes, which emerged in response to the 1930s Great Depression.

Famously, Keynes challenged the notion that in times of crisis the market would automatically return to equilibrium and recovery.

Expansionary policies are necessary to ensure renewed growth—governments need to stimulate demand.

Massive deficit spending was the main policy tool advocated by Keynes to encourage a kickstart to increased investment.

Keynesianism remained the most influential economic theory during the post-war period, until the crises of the 1970s.

Events of 2007–09 led to a resurgence of Keynesianism, with policymakers increasingly turning to expansionary policies to combat the crisis.

What is Marxism?

Whether you love it or hate it, Marxism has been one of the world's most influential ideas over the last century or longer.

Besides its political aspects, Marxism provides a very different understanding of economics from the mainstream point of view.

Every commodity, Marx argued, has a use value and an exchange value. Everything has a purpose and everything costs something!

He argued that labor, too, is a commodity and that it is this feature that is crucial to the growth of capitalism.

The use value of labor is the ability to produce other commodities. The exchange value is the fair price—or wage—paid by the employer.

Yet when this use value is combined with the employer's machines, a surplus is generated that exceeds this fair price.

This surplus is the profits by which capitalism can grow, and their extraction is what Marx refers to as "exploitation."

The expansion of this exploitation, he claimed, produced the antagonisms that would ultimately lead to the overthrow of capitalism.

What is institutionalism?

The main concern of institutionalism is (as we might assume) with institutions—the frameworks within which economic activity is embedded.

The first institutional economists rejected neo-classical economics' concern with general principles of the market or economic behavior.

They argued that economic institutions evolve through history to give an economy its historical and cultural specificity.

For example, the distinctive Federal Reserve System has been shaped by the history of the U.S., while actively shaping its economy.

New institutional economics (NIE) is also mainly concerned with institutions, but with a very different focus.

These economists accept the neo-classical framework and argue that institutions support the natural functioning of the market.

What is dependency theory?

Dependency theory argues that it is the economic relations between rich and poor countries that block the opportunities for development.

It came to prominence in Latin America during the 1950s and 60s as people in the region tried to understand the lack of industrialization.

Centuries of exploitation by wealthy countries, it was alleged, had forced developing countries into a situation of dependency.

The nature of production and exchange means that any and all gains will be made by the rich countries of the core and their corporations.

Poor countries have been integrated into the international economy as suppliers of cheap labor and raw materials.

The peripheral status of these countries within the global system has led to persistent poverty and inequality.

Only a radical break with this system of exploitation can bring about development—anything from tariffs on trade to social revolution!

What is imperialism?

The first things that come to mind about imperialism are vast territorial empires carved out through military force.

While the empires of the Romans, Ottomans, or British have no real parallel today, imperialism is still an important idea.

Rather than these formal empires, it is claimed that the economic relations of international capitalism have created informal empires.

Multinational corporations and global finance provide a new form of power, by seizing control of foreign assets without the need for war.

Market power instead of military power is central to this type of imperialism, but force is never totally absent.

As Venezuelan President Hugo Chavez said, "When imperialism feels weak, it resorts to brute force."

 # What is socialism?

Socialism is a theory of economic organization and production that provides perhaps the most well-known alternative to capitalism.

Socialists argue that the elimination of private property and exploitation would lead to a fairer distribution of work and wealth.

"From each according to his ability, to each according to his need" was the famous slogan Karl Marx used to capture this vision.

The Soviet Union and other communist states around the world sought to implement this alternative system throughout the twentieth century.

Inspired by Marxist theory, these countries used central planning and state ownership as the main tools to tackle capitalist inequality.

Yet the resulting centralization of power, for some, undermined the principles of socialism and, for others, discredited the theory.

What is Taylorism?

Taylorism, or scientific management, was a method of organizing work to maximize the productivity of the workforce.

Named after its pioneer, Frederick Taylor, this theory argued that productivity increases come with precise management of the work process.

Selection, training, and supervision were the three most important areas in Taylor's 1911 book *The Principles of Scientific Management.*

Select the right person for the job: "The workman ... best suited to handling pig iron is unable to understand [its] ... science."

Each employee would then be trained in the most efficient means of carrying out his or her tasks—those tried and tested by management.

Management supervision is the key to making this process work—the monitoring of work practices ensuring that no work time is wasted.

What is Fordism?

Fordism was the pioneering approach behind what we know today as mass production. The Model-T Ford car was the first mass-produced product.

Standardization was central to Fordism, both in terms of the product and the method of production.

Henry Ford famously said, "Any customer can have a car painted any color that he wants, so long as it is black."

The production of standard products reduced costs, as did the standardization of production.

Ford introduced the assembly line in the early twentieth century after seeing a similar device in the meatpacking houses in Chicago.

Each worker would be assigned a single repeated task along this production line. This cut costs and maximized productivity.

Ford also introduced higher pay for his workforce to compensate for the unskilled nature of their work, and to create a market for his cheap car!

 # What is lean production?

Lean production, or Toyotism, is an approach that seeks to eliminate all waste from the production process—keeping it lean and mean!

It is known as Toyotism because it was pioneered by Toyota and was behind the success of Japanese growth in the late twentieth century.

Three of the key problems identified were excessive inventory holding, excessive movement of labor, and delays in the production process.

Also, excessive movement of goods, overproduction, overprocessing, and defects were argued to increase waste and costs.

Just-in-time production was the most famous aspect—parts and products would only be delivered when and where they were needed.

Automation and the use of high-tech production also reduced costs by limiting defects and improving the productivity of the assembly line.

The big thinkers

Ideas don't come from nowhere. During the past 250 years, the field of economics has been shaped by famous figures such as Adam Smith, John Maynard Keynes, Karl Marx, and many lesser known characters. Their influence continues to this day.

Who was
Adam Smith?

The "father of modern economics" was professor of philosophy at Glasgow University.

Smith noted that shopkeepers sell their wares not out of altruism but just to make a living. Yet, their selfishness serves all of society.

It is the "invisible hand" of the market that ensures that exactly the right amount and variety of goods are produced for society's needs.

Smith noted that competition ensures the customer pays the lowest price for a product. In this way, the free market optimizes production.

He spent ten years writing *The Wealth of Nations*, which was published in 1776.

His ideas have been seized upon by free marketeers, but Smith believed that some government intervention was required to keep markets fair.

He railed against monopolies and employers colluding to keep wages down.

Who was
David Ricardo?

David Ricardo was a London stockbroker who "systemized" economics and laid the foundations for classical economic theory.

He made a fortune speculating on the stock market and got interested in economics later in life after reading Smith's *The Wealth of Nations*.

He first rose to fame when he blamed the government for creating inflation by printing too much money. This was the start of monetarism.

His theory of comparative advantage proved that trading partners benefit from trade, even if one country is less efficient than the other.

He also came up with the theory of diminishing returns, which explains why costs increase disproportionately as production levels rise.

Born a Sephardic Jew, he turned his back on his religion and family to marry a pretty Quaker girl. He later became a member of Parliament.

 # Who was J. S. Mill?

John Stuart Mill was the oldest son of the economist/philosopher James Mill who hot-housed him to become a great intellect.

Mill advocated a free market and believed governments should intervene only to prevent people from harming others (the "harm principle").

He also believed that society should act to bring about the greatest happiness to the greatest number of people, known as "utilitarianism."

A great supporter of freedom of speech, he detested censorship and believed that all ideas, however abhorrent, should be openly discussed.

Mill was an early advocate of women's rights and worker's cooperatives. He even suggested reducing economic growth to save the environment.

His most famous published works were *Principles of Political Economy* (1848) and *On Liberty* (1859).

Who was Karl Marx?

Karl Marx was a German philosopher whose ideas formed the basis of the communist revolutions at the beginning of the twentieth century.

Marx believed that all history was about class struggle.

Capitalism can only make a profit by exploiting workers; this will only change by workers taking over the means of production—by force.

All political systems run their course. Just as capitalism replaced feudalism, so communism will replace capitalism. It's a matter of time.

As capitalism heads toward monopoly, this makes it easier to take over the means of production. Thus, it contributes to its own downfall.

Marx married Jenny von Westphalen in 1843 and had seven children by her. He died in near poverty in Hampstead, London, in March 1883.

Although relatively unknown in his own lifetime, Marx's ideas acquired global importance after the Bolshevik Revolution in Russia in 1917.

Who was Alfred Marshall?

While economics was in its infancy, Alfred Marshall gave the subject a more scientific basis by applying rigorous math.

At the same time, he was anxious to make the subject accessible to a wider audience, so he buried most of his math in copious footnotes.

Marshall pioneered the supply and demand theory, which says that the price and output of a product are determined by its supply and demand.

He showed that the market price for a product is where the demand and supply curves meet.

He also came up with the idea of marginal utility, which is the point at which any increase in price will lead to a reduction in sales.

He also introduced price elasticity, which explains why small price changes will affect the sales of some products more than others. Phew!

He took ten years to write his definitive *Principles of Economics*, published in 1890. He died in 1924, before he could finish the follow-up.

Who was Max Weber?

Although now regarded as a founding father of sociology, in his own lifetime Max Weber was primarily known as an economist.

He contended that economics could not be discussed in the abstract and had to take into account human nature.

He devised several "ideal types" to interpret human behavior. This later became the basis for "rational economic man," or *homo economicus*.

In *The Protestant Ethic* and *The Spirit of Capitalism* he argued that Protestants were better adapted to capitalism than Catholics.

Elsewhere, he described government as the only institution that claims a "monopoly on the legitimate use of violence."

Who was John Maynard Keynes?

John Maynard Keynes was a professor of economics at Cambridge University, who advocated government intervention in the economy.

He refuted the idea that free markets eventually lead to full employment by saying: "In the long run, we are all dead."

And, breaking with classical orthodoxy, he insisted the economy is driven by demand, not supply.

He advocated "counter-cyclical" government intervention, i.e., spending more when the economy is weak and less when it is strong.

His ideas were adopted by most Western governments after World War II.

But his policies failed to solve the problem of "stagflation" —a mix of stagnation and inflation—in the 1970s, and fell out of favor.

Keynesianism made a comeback in the 2000s in the stimulus packages implemented by Barack Obama, Gordon Brown, and others.

Who was Friedrich Hayek?

Hayek was an Austrian economist whose ideas provided the intellectual underpinning for the policies of Margaret Thatcher and Ronald Reagan.

His book *The Road to Serfdom* (1944) argues that centrally planned (socialist) economies lead to a loss of personal freedom.

He was widely criticized for his support of the Pinochet government in Chile in the 1970s and 1980s—responsible for the deaths of thousands.

He said it would be better to live under a dictatorship that allowed freedom of choice than under a democracy that didn't.

Hayek became a British citizen in 1938, but moved to Chicago in 1950. He was awarded the Nobel Prize in 1974 and died in 1992.

He continued writing stinging critiques of socialism well into his late eighties. His legacy lives on to this day.

Who was Karl Polanyi?

Karl Polanyi was a maverick Austrian economist who provided the intellectual counterpoint to Friedrich Hayek.

He argued that capitalism was not a natural state but was born of the bourgeoisie's determination to maintain their privileged position.

Unlike previous systems, which were "embedded" within society, capitalism was imposed by the advent of the Industrial Revolution.

Without government intervention to moderate its effects, capitalism destroys normal human relations and devours the environment.

His book *The Great Transformation* was published in 1944 to great acclaim, and still makes for powerful reading.

Polanyi was a cavalry officer in the Austro-Hungarian army during World War I.

He was offered a job at Columbia University in 1947 but was refused a visa because of his wife's communist past. So he commuted from Canada.

Who was Hyman Minsky?

Hyman Minsky was an American economist who described the 2007 credit crunch forty years before it happened.

He believed that boom leads to bust because investors get complacent, take greater risks, and end up borrowing more than they can afford.

He identified three types of borrowers: hedge, speculative, and Ponzi.

Hedge borrowers pay off interest and capital; speculators pay off interest only; Ponzi borrowers rely on appreciation of assets to pay debts.

When the Ponzi borrower defaults, it sets off a chain reaction and banks stop lending even to hedge borrowers. This is a "Minsky moment."

Unlike most economists, who believe markets are inherently stable, Minsky believed human nature makes the cycle of boom and bust inevitable.

He opposed deregulation of financial markets in the 1980s, believing it would encourage excessive risk taking.

Who was Milton Friedman?

According to *The Economist* magazine, Milton Friedman was the most influential economist of the second half of the twentieth century.

Initially a fan of Keynes, he led the backlash in the 1960s, arguing that controlling money supply was more important than public spending.

He was a staunch advocate of free markets and believed in keeping government intervention to an absolute minimum.

As adviser to Ronald Reagan and a key figure in the so-called "Washington Consensus," he led the drive for market deregulation in the 1980s.

He became a household name in the U.S. when he and his wife Rose co-wrote the TV series and best-selling book *Free to Choose*.

He was awarded the Nobel Prize for Economics in 1976 and the Presidential Medal of Freedom by Ronald Reagan in 1988. He died in 2006.

 # Who is Gary Becker?

Gary Becker is an American economist who applied economic theories to areas usually linked to sociology, e.g., families, race, and crime.

Becker's first major work was on racial issues. He discovered that people charge more if selling to someone from a different ethnic group.

He is best known for his "bad kid theorem," which says that even bad kids will treat their siblings well if they know they stand to benefit.

Also, wealthy couples are more likely to stay together than poor ones because the cost of getting a divorce is so much greater.

As more women go to work, the value of their time increases, as does the apparent cost of raising a child. This leads to a lower birth rate.

Becker's views gradually gained credence during his lifetime and are now widely accepted. He received the Nobel Prize for Economics in 1992.

Unreal money

Not all economics relates to production and employment. Equally important are the money markets, which provide the funding for most large businesses nowadays. How an apple-growing company performs on the money markets can be more important than how it performs in the fruit market.

What are stocks and shares?

If a company needs to raise money, one common solution is to issue stocks and sell them to investors. Stocks are also called "equity."

"Stock" is the general term, while "share" is specific: You can own stocks from many companies, or you can own shares in Starbucks.

Companies that offer shares for the public to buy are called public companies. Some have millions of outstanding shares.

When investors buy stocks, they own a fraction of the business. This is called an equity stake and means they can vote at annual meetings.

They also receive a share of the profits as payments called dividends, which are paid once or twice a year to shareholders.

Share values rise or fall depending on company performance, news reports, dividends, future expected earnings, and stock market sales.

What are bonds?

Issuing bonds is another way for a company to finance its business. Cities and governments also use them to raise money.

Unlike stocks, where investors buy a stake in a company, bonds are loans: Investors lend money and expect repayment on a set maturity date.

They also earn fixed amounts of interest at set intervals, unlike stocks, which can be cashed in anytime but don't have a guaranteed value.

In the long run, investors can make much more money from stocks than bonds. However, bonds have advantages.

Repayment is almost guaranteed, interest is paid at regular intervals, and government or municipality bond interest does not get taxed.

Stocks and bonds are types of securities, a word for any investment instrument that represents ownership or debt.

What are stock markets?

Stock markets connect people who have money to invest with people who need money, helping companies and the economy to grow.

Some trading is done at physical stock exchanges and some is done electronically, but "the stock market" describes all these transactions.

The stock market has a lot of liquidity, because stocks can be bought and sold quickly and often, unlike investments such as real estate.

When a market is "up"—a bull market—stock prices are rising; when it's "down"—a bear market—prices are falling.

In theory, the stock market allocates capital where it is needed, and stock prices accurately reflect the underlying values of companies.

But investors, pressured to make short-term gains, often buy what's going up now, overvaluing the asset and inflating market levels.

This "herd mentality" can create speculative bubbles, like the dot-com bubble of the late 1990s—and crashes can hurt.

A country's stock market is considered an important signal of its economic strength.

What are derivatives?

Buying a derivative is like placing a bet. Why? A derivative has no value of its own—its value depends on the outcome of something else.

That value can come from many things: gold prices, interest rates, the stock market, loan defaults, or even other derivatives.

If your friend pays you $10 to promise you'll buy him a beer every time it goes above 90 degrees in July—that's a derivative.

The derivatives market is worth hundreds of trillions of dollars, over 10 times as much as the world economy.

Investors use derivatives to insure against risk (by hedging) or take on risk to profit (through speculation).

Though some, like futures, have been around for a long time, in recent years very complicated and risky derivatives have been developed.

Investor Warren Buffett called them "financial weapons of mass destruction," because a few big losses can trigger a financial crisis.

What are futures?

Futures are a type of derivative, created in the 1850s, to protect agricultural producers and buyers from changing prices.

Several months in advance, a seller and buyer agree to exchange something (like a set amount of grain) on a set date at a set price.

It reduces risk: If market prices ("spot prices") drop, farmers won't lose money; if market prices rise, buyers won't have to pay too much.

People began buying futures with no intent to sell or buy grain, settling the difference in cash—in other words, speculating for profit.

In 1972, currency futures were invented, with similar logic: they protect investors from shifting exchange rates and allow speculation.

Since then, futures have also been created for other commodities like oil, interest rates, stock indices—even foreign governments' debt.

Unlike some financial transactions, futures have standardized terms, are regulated by agencies, and are traded in clearing houses.

 # What is speculation?

Speculation is buying, selling, or holding financial securities (like stocks, bonds, or futures) to profit from price fluctuations.

Speculative trading is usually short-term, and it's a risky practice, with the potential for huge gains—or huge losses.

Speculation often involves start-up companies, or volatile commodities like oil, where investors profit by betting on future prices.

Speculators often use leverage, borrowing money to invest. Investing borrowed money can increase returns, but can also lead to huge losses.

Smart investors hedge: They take positions that will offset each other to limit potential losses, but this also limits potential gains.

What is hedging?

Investors use hedging to reduce their exposure to risk. This is done by making an investment that reduces the risk of another investment.

Hedging, also known as "offsetting" risk, protects investors against potential losses, but it also limits potential profits.

For example, if an investor buys stock, he can also buy a futures contract that allows him to sell stock at a set price on a set date.

This way, if stock prices fall dramatically, it reduces his risk of loss—but if they rise a lot, hedging limits the gains he can make.

Exporters hedge against currency fluctuations, banks hedge against credit defaulters, and airlines hedge against rising fuel prices.

Many kinds of financial instruments and techniques are used to hedge, such as futures, swaps, options, insurance policies, and short-selling.

What is a commodity market?

Commodity markets are for trading futures in raw or primary products, like oil, copper, gold, corn, wheat, coffee, and cocoa.

You can't trade whatever or whenever you want. Commodity market trading takes place on commodity exchanges, which are regulated.

The exchanges set standard quantities for trading, and the commodity has to be on a list: About one hundred are traded worldwide.

Trades rarely end in someone actually delivering oil or corn. Usually, people trade the contracts, or "close out," i.e., cash them in.

Commodity futures affect the economy by making price predictions public. When oil prices rise, the prices of goods and services rise too.

Large-scale trade can even change prices: If you buy many oil futures above market price, producers hoard to earn more for their oil later.

The speculation becomes a self-fulfilling prophecy: hoarding reduces the oil supply, and the oil price goes up.

 # What are money markets?

Money markets trade in short-term debt securities, like certificates of deposit or Treasury bonds, which mature in less than a year.

Money market investments are very conservative and safe. There's little risk of losing your money, so returns are low.

However, since you can withdraw money at any time, it's useful for large institutions and governments to manage short-term cash needs.

Unlike the stock market, most money market securities trade in high amounts, so most trading is done between banks.

However, ordinary investors can buy into a money market fund, where thousands of investors' money is pooled to buy money market securities.

Money markets are better for wealthy investors, because the more money deposited, the higher the interest rate.

What is a mutual fund?

Mutual funds are a way for many investors to pool their money to buy stocks, bonds, and other securities.

Like stocks, investors buy and sell mutual fund shares and earn dividends each year, but the shares represent a "basket" of securities.

Most mutual funds have a professional fund manager who decides what securities to buy and sell in order to maximize growth.

Mutual funds may invest in stocks, bonds, or other securities, at home or abroad, with varying risk levels, to meet different goals.

Investors are charged an expense ratio to pay managers and administrative costs, usually 0.5 to 1.5 percent of the fund's assets.

Past performance doesn't predict future results: Mutual funds that profited in the past may not do well in the future.

Since transaction costs are shared and a professional manager's in charge, most people invest in mutual funds instead of directly in stocks.

What is a hedge fund?

Hedge funds are mutual funds for rich people: To buy in, you need a minimum net worth of at least $1 million and strong investing knowledge.

They are lightly regulated, with fewer restrictions on using derivatives and leverage; many are offshore to avoid taxes.

Hedge funds try to make money even when the market's falling, and they use complicated financial techniques to achieve that goal.

One of these techniques is leverage: borrowing money to make the fund bigger. This means bigger profits, but can also mean bigger losses.

Since they use so much leverage, hedge funds are riskier than other funds, and critics say that they lack transparency.

Profits depend heavily on a manager's skill, so the manager is paid a performance fee, usually 10 to 25 percent of profits.

What are blue-chip companies?

If you're going to buy stock, it's usually good to invest in a blue-chip company—if you can afford it.

Blue-chip companies are large, successful companies with a good profit record, well-known for high-quality products.

They've generally been in business for a long time, are usually international, and have weathered bad times to come out on top.

Examples of blue-chip companies in the U.S. are IBM, McDonald's, Coca-Cola, Exxon Mobil, Walt Disney, Kraft, AT&T, and Microsoft.

The name comes from gambling: Just as blue chips are the most valuable chips in poker, blue-chip company stocks are a valuable investment.

Blue-chip companies are considered less risky than small or new companies, so their stock sells at a high price.

However, blue-chip companies can still perform badly: After over 80 years as a blue-chip stock, General Motors filed for bankruptcy.

What is the Dow Jones?

The Dow Jones Industrial Average is the average stock price of thirty blue-chip American companies.

It's an example of a market index, an instrument used to figure out the overall health of the economy.

Each market index tracks a "basket" of securities, like stocks, bonds, or futures. Some follow a specific industry, like energy.

The Dow, a stock index, tracks the stock prices of thirty leading companies, including AT&T, Bank of America, Microsoft, and McDonald's.

The Dow is quoted more than any other index. When it goes up, it signals that the economy's doing well; when it goes down, it's a bad sign.

The average is quoted in points, with eight points to the dollar, using a formula that adjusts when companies issue more stocks.

Knowing the average is useful for investors, who can compare specific stocks to the average in order to make investment decisions.

What is the NASDAQ?

The NASDAQ was created in 1971. It was the first electronic stock exchange in the world, so it never had a physical trading floor.

It provides stock price quotes, which are constantly changing, and uses a computer to connect buyers and sellers when their prices match.

The NASDAQ has more trading volume than any other stock exchange in the world, with about 3,700 companies listed for trade.

It's often associated with high-tech stocks and new companies, and trades over-the-counter stocks that aren't listed on other exchanges.

The NASDAQ offers after-hours trading. This helps investors react quickly to news, but after-hours prices are more volatile.

The NASDAQ Composite Index, which tracks stock traded on NASDAQ, is generally used to track the health of the technology sector.

 # What is an index fund?

An index fund is a type of mutual fund that follows a market index, like the Dow Jones or the S&P 500.

Unlike actively managed mutual funds, which try to beat the market, index funds simply try to mirror market performance.

Index funds invest in the same stocks as a market index, in the same proportions. When the market changes, these allocations stay the same.

This passive management doesn't need expensive analysts and trades less frequently, which means its overhead costs are much lower.

The result? Even though actively managed funds try to beat the market, index funds usually outperform managed funds in the long run.

What are credit ratings?

Credit ratings evaluate governments and businesses that issue debt (like bonds), and rate them on how likely they are to pay back that debt.

Ratings can range from AAA, for very financially stable companies, to D, for companies defaulting on debt.

Investors rely on credit ratings to make decisions, so if you want people to invest in your business, a good rating is vital.

Companies with a high rating pay less interest on a loan, since they're trusted to pay back the loan.

Ratings are done by ratings agencies, like Moody's or Standard and Poor's, which interview executives and review company data.

Agencies make mistakes: They gave an AAA rating to the risky mortgage-backed securities that helped cause the 2007–09 financial crisis.

What is shareholder value?

Technically, shareholder value is the value a shareholder earns from investing in a company—in other words, dividend payments on stock.

More broadly, however, the term stands for a philosophy of business management, or "corporate governance," that emerged in the 1980s.

According to the shareholder value doctrine, a company is successful if it has high stock values and pays big dividends to shareholders.

The focus on rewarding shareholders means companies pay out their profits as dividends, instead of reinvesting in equipment or employees.

In sum, by adopting shareholder value, companies changed their profit strategy from "retain and reinvest" to "downsize and distribute."

Critics point out a dark side: If companies pay workers less, they can pay shareholders more, enriching the few at the expense of the many.

Critics also point out that executives are often paid in stocks, not just in salaries—and thus may benefit most from shareholder value.

 # What are stock options?

Stock options give employees the right to buy a set number of shares of their company's stock at a specific time and price.

The period of time that employees must hold the stock options before they are allowed to buy stock is called the "vesting period."

Because employees benefit if stock prices rise, stock options give them an incentive to work hard, so the company's value will increase.

However, stock options can end up worthless, or "underwater," if a company's not doing well—a common problem during the dot-com bust.

CEOs often have thousands or tens of thousands of stock options, and corrupt CEOs may artificially inflate stock prices before cashing in.

Stock options are criticized for widening the gap between the rich and the rest: since the 1970s, CEO pay quadrupled while real wages fell.

What is short-selling?

Short-selling is a way to profit in the market, even when stock prices are falling.

"Going short" is the opposite of "going long," the more common way to invest, where the investor profits if the security price goes up.

To short sell, you borrow stocks that you don't have and sell them at the current market price—say, 100 stocks at $10 a share, for $1,000.

To repay the stocks you borrowed, you buy them back at a later date. If the price is down to $7 a share, you pay $700, and earn $300 profit.

It's risky: If the stock price rises after all, it will cost more money to buy them back, and you'll lose money on the deal.

The terms "shorting" or "going short" also refer to any derivative contract where the investor profits when asset prices fall.

What is an investment bank?

Unlike retail banks, which accept cash deposits and give loans, investment banks sell and manage securities, like stocks or derivatives.

Investment banks act as intermediaries to help companies or governments raise money—a process called "underwriting."

For example, if a private company wants to sell stocks, it can sell them to an investment bank, which then sells them to the public.

Investment banks, like Goldman Sachs or J. P. Morgan Chase, also give advice on business mergers and acquisitions, and help facilitate them.

They can also act as a broker for institutions: A company lets the investment bank manage its assets in order to earn good returns.

In order to make a profit, the investment bank buys and sells financial products—often very complex and risky derivatives.

The 2007–09 credit crisis was largely caused by investment banks, which speculated heavily, using lots of leverage, on risky securities.

 # What is ethical investing?

Ethical investing, also called socially responsible investing, aims to maximize social good in addition to financial gain.

It's done in several ways. One is negative screening—avoiding certain investments, like tobacco or weapons, because of ethical concerns.

Ethical investing also takes the form of divesting: removing investments from a portfolio because of ethical concerns.

Positive investing is when people invest in companies that are doing good things, in fields like alternative energy and green building.

Advocates argue that ethical investing earns good returns, both in the short and long term—you don't have to give up wealth for morals.

Most major investment organizations offer an "ethical" fund, although how ethical these funds truly are is a much-debated matter.

Boom and bust

In a free market economy, prices are allowed to find their own level. This means that you often have a speculative bubble followed by a crash. Some boom-and-bust cycles are more dangerous than others. So what can be done to stabilize the markets?

What is a bubble?

A bubble is the overvaluation of an asset (e.g., stocks and property), followed by a sudden devaluation, known as a crash.

Recent examples are the 1990s dot-com bubble and the 2000s property bubble. The first ever bubble was Tulip Mania in Holland in the 1730s.

No one really knows why they occur. Some say it's for the same reasons as inflation, i.e., there's too much money in the economy.

When interest rates are low, people tend to spend instead of saving money, leading to a spending bubble. And it's cheap to borrow more.

According to the "greater fool theory," people (fools) pay over the odds for an asset if they think they can sell it on to a greater fool.

During a bubble, holders of overvalued assets have an artificial sense of wealth, which encourages them to spend beyond their means.

What is a recession?

A recession is when Gross Domestic Product falls for at least two quarters in a row, or unemployment rises by 1.5 percent a year.

The National Bureau of Economic Research in the U.S. decides when it's a recession. Its analysis includes factors such as income.

Recessions are characterized by a reduction in consumer spending and capital investment, and a rise in unemployment and bankruptcies.

The good news is that they are usually also accompanied by a fall in the rate of inflation.

Governments counter recessions by either increasing the flow of money (monetarism) and/or increasing government spending (Keynesianism).

A recession is often preceded by a growth accompanied by high unemployment, volatile share prices, and a lack of new business creation.

What is boom and bust?

Boom and bust is when an economy expands dramatically, only to contract again. It's a bubble followed by a recession.

Boom and bust cycles are usually caused by unsustainable growth fueled by an increase in the price of an asset beyond its realistic value.

Some estimates say the U.S. has experienced thirty-two cycles of boom and bust in the past 150 years—averaging one every 4½ years.

The most famous example is the boom of the Roaring Twenties followed by the stock market crash of 1929 and the Great Depression.

Keynes thought he had conquered the cycle in the 1950s. So did Bill Clinton in the 1990s. And Gordon Brown in the 2000s. None really had.

The 2000s boom was caused by an overreliance on consumer spending to fuel growth. When people stopped spending, the bust soon followed.

What is liquidity?

Liquidity is the ability of an asset to be sold with minimum loss of value. For this to happen, there must be a ready pool of buyers.

The easier an asset is to sell, the more "liquid" it is. Cash is the most liquid asset of all.

In business, liquidity refers to the ability of a company to keep its current account in credit and pay its debts on time.

If too much is invested in stock and capital assets, it won't be able to pay its debts. It may then have a liquidation sale to raise funds.

Banks are required by law to maintain a certain amount of liquidity. The exact amount has varied over time and is often disputed.

A "liquidity trap" is when investment in the economy dries up, despite low interest rates and huge injections of cash from the government.

It is said to have happened in the U.S. in the 1930s and Japan in the 1990s.

What is insolvency?

Insolvency is the inability of a person or company to pay their debts. There are two types: cash flow insolvency and balance sheet insolvency.

Cash flow insolvency is when there's not enough liquidity to pay debts; balance sheet insolvency is when debts outweigh assets (i.e., equity).

It's possible for a company to be solvent on paper, but not be able to realize enough liquidity (i.e. cash) to pay off its immediate debts.

It's also possible for a company to be able to pay off its debts, thanks to a healthy cash flow, while being insolvent on paper.

A company that is insolvent isn't necessarily bankrupt. Most countries have measures to allow companies time to restructure their debts.

If this doesn't work, then a company can be put into liquidation. This can be done voluntarily by shareholders or forced by creditors.

 # What is bankruptcy?

Bankruptcy is the legal declaration of a company's or individual's inability to pay their debts. In the U.K. it refers to individuals only.

Once a person/company is declared bankrupt, their assets are seized and sold to pay debts. The individuals concerned are no longer liable.

Under the U.S. Federal Bankruptcy Code, there are six ways a person or company can be declared bankrupt, each known by a different "chapter."

Chapter 11 is known as "corporate bankruptcy," since it allows companies to carry on trading while they restructure their debts.

Although originally designed to ensure that creditors received their due, bankruptcy laws are increasingly used to protect debtors from ruin.

But bankruptcy still carries social stigma and may bar individuals from certain activities, such as holding public office.

What is nationalization?

Nationalization is when a national government takes over a private company and places it in public ownership.

This often happens because the company is about to go bust and the government thinks it's essential for the economy to keep it going.

Or it can be for political reasons. Most socialists believe certain key services should be run for the public good rather than private gain.

Previous owners of nationalized companies are usually paid compensation. In extreme examples, they may not be; this is called "expropriation."

After the Castro revolution in Cuba, all foreign-owned companies were expropriated by the government. Only a few were compensated.

Common targets for nationalization are infrastructure providers, such as water, electricity, post offices, and public transportation.

What is a bailout?

A bailout is when a company is given credit to prevent it from going bankrupt, usually because it can't pay bills due to a lack of liquidity.

Bailouts are mainly given by the government, but one company can bail out another—although here the aim is usually to take over a competitor.

If many jobs and businesses are dependent on a company, then government might think it's "too big to fail" and step in to save it.

In exchange, the government usually receives shares in the company, which it can sell at a later date to recoup some of its expenditure.

Free-marketeers believe that bailouts encourage businesses to take excessive risk knowing that the government will step in if it goes wrong.

Banks around the world were bailed out in 2007–09 because they were deemed "too big to fail," costing taxpayers many billions of dollars.

 # What is a stimulus?

A stimulus is when government attempts to revive a faltering economy by increasing the amount of money in the system.

This can be done through monetary policy (lower interest rates) or fiscal policy (higher government spending).

For decades, economists have advocated a monetarist approach because it minimizes the role of government and interferes less with markets.

During the 2007–09 crisis, many governments had lowered their interest rates to nearly 0 percent, forcing them to adopt a fiscal approach.

The idea is that government spending replaces consumer spending and is recouped in increased tax revenue and lower unemployment benefits.

The trouble with stimulus spending is it saddles a country with debts that have to be paid by taxpayers. It also smacks of "big government."

What is leverage?

In finance, leverage means using debt (e.g., borrowing through instruments such as futures and options) to expand an investment.

The greater the leverage, the greater the amount borrowed, and the greater the potential return—but also the greater the potential loss.

What starts as a small-risk investment expands through leverage and, if it fails, results in an expanded loss.

High levels of leverage were partly responsible for the 2007–09 crisis because they magnified companies' losses.

In business, leverage is the amount of debt used to finance a company. A company with a lot of debt is said to be "highly leveraged."

You can work out a company's leverage by dividing the amount it owes by the amount it has in assets. The result is its "leverage ratio."

A high leverage ratio suggests a company is borrowing more than it can really afford and is therefore not a good investment option.

What are asset-backed securities?

Asset-backed securities (ABSs) are shares based on a pool of assets, not a single asset, such as shares in a company.

The pool is usually made up of "illiquid" assets that would otherwise be hard to sell, such as mortgages, car loans, and student loans.

By "bundling" them together, the risk from individual assets is reduced and they become a financial product that can be bought and sold.

"Securitization" also frees original lenders from liability, freeing up capital and allowing them to lend more.

The process took off in the 1980s, and as brokers were rewarded for quantity rather than quality, lending criteria became increasingly lax.

When too many "subprime" borrowers defaulted on payments, the value of these ABSs plummeted, sending the financial institutions into crisis.

The result was the 2007 credit crunch and the ensuing crisis of 2007–09.

What is a credit default swap?

A credit default swap (CDS) is effectively an insurance against a financial product, such as a bond or loan, defaulting.

The buyer pays premiums to the seller and, if the bond defaults, receives a lump sum. If it doesn't default, the seller keeps the premiums.

CDSs are bought by investors wanting to manage risk: if the bond behaves normally they make money; if it defaults they make money too.

CDSs are also bought by speculators who believe a bond will default. In this respect, CDSs are more like gambling.

Since the size of the premium is determined by the perceived risk of a bond, CDSs are seen as providing a good measure of creditworthiness.

Collapse of banks such as Lehman Brothers has been blamed on high CDS risk ratings leading to general loss of confidence.

What are CDOs?

Collateralized Debt Obligations (CDOs) are asset-backed securities, meaning they are based on a pool of assets rather than a single asset.

What makes CDOs unique is that the packages are cut up into "tranches" and sold according to the degree of risk associated with them.

These range from senior (least risk) to junior (most risk). Profits are paid in order of seniority, while losses are borne first by juniors.

So junior tranches protect senior ones by absorbing losses. On the other hand, the higher the risk, the bigger the pay-outs.

CDOs were created in 1987. A decade later they were the fastest-growing sector of the market.

They were so complex that many investors didn't understand what they were buying. By 2008, most CDO traders required massive bailouts.

In October 2007, Merrill Lynch reported quarterly losses of $7.9 billion on CDOs alone. A year later, it was bought out by Bank of America.

What were SIVs?

Structured Investment Vehicles (SIVs) were a financial product invented by Citigroup in the 1980s financial boom.

Their model was to take out short-term loans at low rates of interest and invest in long-term financial products with high rates of return.

The difference between the two rates yielded a profit. This also meant SIVs had to refinance regularly to maintain their investments.

SIVs invested mainly in asset-backed securities, which included mortgages in their portfolios, including subprime mortgages.

When short-term loans dried up in 2007, SIVs were unable to refinance their long-term investments before they reached maturity.

By the end of 2008, the product no longer existed.

 # What are Fannie Mae and Freddie Mac?

Fannie Mae and Freddie Mac are both privately (i.e., shareholder) owned businesses that provide finance for American mortgage lenders.

Both companies buy mortgages from lenders and repackage them as bonds, which they sell to investors. This allows lenders to lend more.

Fannie Mae stands for Federal National Mortgage Association; Freddie Mac stands for Federal Home Loan Mortgage Corporation.

Fannie Mae was created by the U.S. government in 1938 to increase the number of mortgages available for homebuyers.

Fannie Mae was privatized in 1968, and Freddie Mac was created in 1970 to provide competition.

By 2007, they funded half of all U.S. mortgages, worth $12 trillion, but lost $3 billion in three months.

In 2008, the U.S. government put both companies under "conservatorship" to prevent them going bust in the wake of the subprime crisis.

Going global

Economies don't
exist in isolation,
especially not in a
globalized world.
Yet some countries
seem to do better
than others in the
world economy.
As in the rest of life,
it's often the rich
and powerful who
get to make the rules.

What is globalization?

Over the past twenty years, goods, services, and capital have become more mobile, and national economies have grown more interlinked.

What's behind it? Many factors. Better communication and transportation help ideas, goods, and people move around the globe.

International agreements encourage trade across borders, and financial capital can invest anywhere in the world.

Globalization's reach is broad: Whether in New York or rural India, it's reshaped the playing field for governments, companies, and people.

Some claim it can bring more prosperity for all; others say it helps the rich and hurts the poor. Like it or not, it's here to stay.

What are exchange rates?

An exchange rate is how much one currency is worth compared to another.

Today most rates are "floating" or flexible, but pre-1971, currencies were pegged or "fixed" to the dollar. Some are still pegged today.

Rates are shaped by many factors: interest rates, inflation, supply/demand, and a country's political/economic situation.

When exchange rates float, they can affect the cost of an overseas holiday, but they really make an impact in the foreign exchange market.

The "forex" market was created in the 1970s to help international trade and investment, but it's also used to speculate and profit.

Traders buy and sell large amounts of currencies to profit from changing rates—over $3.2 trillion changes hands per day.

The huge volume of forex trade can affect a currency's worth: If too many investors sell the euro at once, demand drops and its value falls.

What is the balance of payments?

A country's balance of payments is the difference between the amount of money flowing out and the amount coming in.

It has two parts. The current account includes goods, services, investment earnings, and one-way transfers such as remittances or foreign aid.

The capital account includes country-owned assets abroad, foreign-owned assets at home, and financial products like bonds or currencies.

In theory, the balance of payments should be zero, but that never happens. A negative balance means more flows out than in, and vice versa.

When a nation buys more goods and services than it sells, and spending exceeds earning, it has a current account or trade deficit.

To balance a current account deficit, a nation creates a capital account surplus by selling more capital assets (like bonds) than it buys.

Countries with trade deficits, like the U.S., borrow money from abroad to pay for their spending; this draws criticism.

What are capital controls?

When people buy or sell things across national borders, the money moving in and out of a country or currency is known as capital flows.

Capital flows take many forms, like foreign direct investment in a company, or buying and selling real estate, derivatives, or currencies.

Capital flows have benefits: Poor nations can access funding for development, and governments can borrow and lend as needed.

But free capital flows can make countries vulnerable: large inflows may cause inflation and debt, and large outflows can devalue a currency.

To protect its economy, a government can use capital controls, which limit capital flows in and out of a country.

Since the 1970s, mainstream economists have discouraged capital controls, but they may be coming back in style for emerging economies.

Regulating capital flows can prevent speculative attacks, and help countries keep control of domestic monetary policy and unemployment.

What is protectionism?

Protectionism is when governments limit trade between countries to protect businesses and workers at home.

It's the opposite of free trade, when goods and services move freely between nations according to supply and demand.

It can take the form of import quotas, or limits; tariffs, which raise import prices; or subsidies, government payments to help companies.

These policies aim to protect businesses from foreign competition, protect jobs, and ensure national prosperity.

Many economists think protectionist policies hurt more than they help because they distort the market, but they're still very common.

The U.S. and the European Union are often criticized for agricultural subsidies and protectionist policies that harm poor countries' exports.

 # What is the euro?

The euro is the European currency. Introduced in eleven countries in 1999, it is used by sixteen of the twenty-seven EU member states.

The "Eurozone" is the largest example of an optimum currency area, where a region shares one currency to maximize economic efficiency.

The euro saves costs of exchanging currency, removes exchange rate risks, and has increased movement of goods, financial assets, and people.

It's helped weak economies grow stronger, access capital, and attract investment—but to join the club, nations must meet strict criteria.

Some E.U. members, like the U.K., refuse to join because they would lose the ability to set their own interest rates.

Its influence matters: In 2008, the euro passed the U.S. dollar to become the currency with the most cash in circulation.

What is the IMF?

The International Monetary Fund was born in 1944 to watch over and stabilize the international financial system.

It monitors members' economies, especially exchange rates and balance of payments, and gives loans to maintain stability and prevent crises.

Each of its 186 members has a quota, based on its economic size, that determines its subscription fee, voting power, and access to loans.

Part of the fee is paid in Special Drawing Rights, an artificial currency the IMF uses for accounts and to increase global liquidity.

In the 1980s, the IMF also put economic development on its agenda, loaning to poor countries to reduce debt and spur trade and production.

However, its loans come with "conditionalities"—recipients have to follow the IMF's free-market rules, which often hurt more than help.

What is the World Bank?

The World Bank was set up in 1944, along with the IMF, to promote development and reduce poverty.

It makes loans and offers technical expertise to help countries improve health, education, infrastructure, communications, and government.

The World Bank was charged with achieving the United Nations' eight Millennium Development Goals (MDGs) by 2015.

The MDGs include universal primary education, female empowerment, sustainability, fighting HIV and malaria, and eradicating extreme poverty.

Despite these ambitious goals, critics say its free-market, "one-size-fits-all" policies have created more poverty than they've eliminated.

Power is also uneven: Rich countries have more say in the voting process and choose leadership, even though policies mainly affect the poor.

What is the WTO?

The World Trade Organization regulates trade policy between nations to make sure trade flows smoothly, predictably, and freely.

Formerly called the General Agreement on Tariffs and Trade (GATT), the WTO was created in 1995 with a permanent framework and wider reach.

WTO agreements, negotiated by 153 member countries and ratified by their governments, act as legal guidelines for international trade.

If a country violates WTO agreements and refuses to shape up, the complaining country can impose restrictions on trade, called sanctions.

The WTO claims its policies make the economic world more prosperous, peaceful, and accountable, but not everyone agrees.

Its TRIPS agreement, which enforces intellectual property rights, means poor countries often can't afford patent-protected drugs.

What is the gold standard?

The gold standard is a system of fixed exchange rates: countries agree to fix their currency values to a set price for gold.

From 1879 to 1914, many modern trading nations used the gold standard to balance trade accounts, but it fell apart when war broke out.

It was adopted again in 1946. This time the price of gold was fixed at $35 an ounce, and countries could trade gold for U.S. dollars.

It creates stability, but it has downsides: If rates are fixed, countries can't manipulate them to tackle inflation, unemployment, or crisis.

The U.S. dropped the gold standard in 1971 due to inflation—there wasn't enough gold to back up the increasing global money supply.

Today we use fiat money, which isn't fixed to any object. It has worth because governments guarantee it and everyone believes in it.

What was Bretton Woods?

In 1944, forty-four countries met in Bretton Woods, New Hampshire, to rebuild the post-war economy and international economic cooperation.

The meeting was the first time nations set up rules, institutions, and procedures to govern the international monetary system.

Past experience showed that cooperation was needed, so the conference established the IMF and World Bank, and restored the gold standard.

The Bretton Woods system was designed to be multilateral, but in practice it was largely directed by the U.S., its most powerful member.

The system was optimistic: It assumed the IMF could offer enough liquidity to cope with crises and that accounts would mainly be balanced.

But structural changes, inflation, and its trade deficit forced the U.S. to drop the gold standard in 1971—the end of Bretton Woods.

 # What is the OECD?

The Organization for Economic Cooperation and Development is a group of thirty countries working to promote democracy and the market economy.

It was set up in 1961, and broadened to include non-European countries like the U.S. and Japan.

It's a rich country club: Most members are wealthy—or getting there—like Mexico, Poland, and Turkey.

OECD goals include sustainable economic growth, high employment, financial stability, growth in world trade, and helping countries develop.

It's an important source of statistics, and it also predicts and studies changing patterns of things like trade, technology, and taxation.

Chile's entry was ratified in January 2010, making it the thirty-first member—and the first from Latin America.

What is the Washington Consensus?

The Washington Consensus is a set of free-market policy recommendations for developing countries.

Developed in the late 1980s by the IMF and World Bank, it claims that the key to development is deregulation and a balanced budget.

To develop, countries need to stabilize the money supply, keep inflation down, and open their borders to free trade.

Privatizing state-owned businesses, opening borders to foreign investment and multinational business, and balancing the budget are also key.

The Consensus, often used interchangeably with "neo-liberalism," is often blamed for what's gone wrong in the developing world.

Its "one-size-fits-all" policies have been criticized for failing to take specific local conditions into account.

What is structural adjustment?

If the Washington Consensus is a set of guidelines, structural adjustment policies (SAPs) turn those guidelines into requirements.

When poor countries want loans from the IMF or the World Bank, they have to agree to conditions that control how they spend the money.

These conditions broadly follow Washington Consensus principles: stabilize, liberalize, privatize, globalize, and balance the budget.

In theory, pushing poor countries to be more market-oriented will boost trade and production, helping their economies grow.

SAPs have had some positive effects on the balance of payments, but their effects on poverty and human well-being are often criticized.

Many governments have had to slash jobs and spend less on education and health, and steep interest rates often lead to more debt, not less.

 # What happened in Seattle?

When the WTO met in Seattle in 1999, over 50,000 people from eighty-seven countries came to protest against free trade and globalization.

Protesters argued that trade rules are written to help big companies and rich countries, with no regard to human rights or the environment.

They argued that free trade and export-led development increase poverty, worsen labor conditions, and ignore poor countries' voices.

Police used tear gas and rubber bullets and arrested 500 protesters, which drew even more media attention to the protesters' cause.

Inside the talks, Third World WTO delegates also helped thwart the agreements, angry that debate was minimal and agreements were rushed.

The talks failed, but it was a turning point: The Washington Consnsus was seriously challenged and new global activist networks were formed.

What is a multinational?

Multinationals or multinational corporations (MNCs) are companies that have offices or factories in more than one country.

Also known as transnational corporations (TNCs) or multinational enterprises (MNEs), they're powerful players in the world economy.

Today, they're increasingly common: of the 100 largest economies in the world today, more than half are MNCs.

MNCs may set up abroad to create new markets, bypass protectionist laws, save on transportation or labor, and avoid shifting exchange rates.

Critics say they have too much political influence, exploit poor countries' labor and resources, and create job losses at home by outsourcing.

What is "offshore"?

"Offshore" is another word for "tax havens"—countries or territories where taxes are very low or don't exist at all.

Tax havens—usually small, wealthy countries—are also secretive: they protect financial information and lack transparency.

They encourage noncitizens to set up business or register assets within their borders, to avoid taxes and save money.

Today, most offshore economic activity revolves around financial services, like mutual funds, banking, life insurance, and pensions.

For tax havens, attracting business can increase local employment and skills transfer, and bring revenue and growth—even with few taxes.

But critics charge that when billions of dollars in taxes aren't paid, wealthy companies and people avoid their responsibility to society.

The OECD has put pressure on tax havens to crack down on "unfair tax competition." Some laws have changed, but offshore still thrives.

What is the "race to the bottom"?

Countries rich and poor want to attract MNCs because they bring employment, tax revenue, and economic growth.

However, in the age of what's called "footloose capital," when an MNC can set up shop just about anywhere, this can have perverse effects.

The power of MNCs to come and go as they please forces governments to make policies that are good for business, not for people.

To attract MNCs, countries have to compete: They offer lower taxes, cheaper labor, and fewer regulations so companies can expect to profit.

This is called the "race to the bottom"—competitive lowering of regulations that has devastating impacts for workers and the environment.

When production moves to the place with the lowest wages and the fewest workers' rights, it creates a downward socio-economic spiral.

Thanks to the race to the bottom, many jobs have moved from the U.S. and now they're moving from Mexico to China.

What is the military-industrial complex?

The phrase "military-industrial complex" came from President Eisenhower's farewell address in 1961, when he warned against it.

How does it work? The arms industry is a big player in the economy because it buys stuff and funds research, so government subsidizes it.

Often, the government pays far more than it should for products and services, or purchases things it might not need.

Things can get ridiculous: In the Reagan years, one company charged the U.S. military $600 for toilet seats.

If it gets so corrupt, why do lawmakers allow it (or even support it)? Some may profit personally, but for many it helps their districts.

One aircraft has subcontractors in forty-four states. That's money and jobs for a lot of people—and no one wants those jobs to disappear.

Some critics say the military-industrial complex is part of why the U.S. went to war in Iraq: because war pays salaries and lines pockets.

Why is the dollar the world currency?

The dollar's been the de facto world currency since 1946. Its value was fixed to gold, and all other currencies were fixed to the dollar.

Today the dollar isn't pegged to gold, but many countries peg their currencies to it. Some use dollars alongside their own money.

Lots of countries hold dollars in their foreign exchange reserves, so they can use them for international trade in things like oil or gold.

Products traded on a global market are often priced in dollars: in 2008, 68 percent of financial transactions were in dollars.

Critics say this lets the U.S. control other countries' political and economic processes—it's essentially a new form of imperialism.

Some economists want a global currency, run by a central bank. The euro's improving—it was used for 26.5 percent of transactions in 2008.

 # Why is the U.S. in debt?

The U.S. was the world's biggest creditor twenty-five years ago—but trends in the late 1980s and 1990s tipped it into debt.

The U.S. has two kinds of debt. First, it has a government spending deficit, because it spends more than it raises in taxes.

Second, it has a trade deficit, because it imports more than it exports—in other words, it also spends more than it earns in global trade.

If you spend more than you earn, you have to borrow money, so the U.S. issues bonds at home and runs a trade deficit abroad.

For example, if the U.S. buys 2,000 TVs from China, it owes China money, while China is lending money to the U.S.

The trade debt is part of America's current account deficit. It is the largest in the world—over $700 billion in 2008 (5 percent of GDP).

Catching up

What can the poorer countries do to catch up with the developed world? Solutions range from trying to protect local industries through protectionism to opening the doors to foreign investment. Everyone wants economic development, it seems, but at what price?

What is export-led development?

If a country follows an export-led strategy of development it means that international trade is its main source of growth.

Rather than a simple free-trade policy, however, this approach to development requires strong policy support to ensure competitiveness.

The most successful examples of this strategy are the East Asian Tigers—South Korea, Taiwan, Singapore, and Hong Kong.

These countries created low-cost manufacturing industries that supplied competitive exports to the world economy, and grew rapidly.

A focus upon manufactured exports, however, is difficult —new, developing country firms have to compete with well-established global firms.

Many countries then have to rely upon raw material exports that have unstable prices and create far less employment.

What is ISI?

Import-substitution industrialization (ISI) is an approach to development that seeks to promote industry by blocking imports.

This process initially came about as depression and war in the 1930s and 1940s stopped trade, and local entrepreneurs filled the gap.

Later on, this activity was encouraged by policymakers, particularly in the Latin American economies of Argentina, Brazil, and Mexico.

These countries used tariffs, subsidies, state investment, and wage policies to stimulate the growth of industry for the domestic market.

The rationale is that by blocking specific imports and providing subsidies, domestic industry will grow at the expense of foreign firms.

State investment and increasing wages provide for increasing demand that can further stimulate production.

Despite initial success, ISI broke down in the 1970s and 1980s as persistent stagnation and inflation undermined the approach.

 # What is sustainable development?

The debate on sustainable development looks beyond simply the need for economic growth—it raises questions for our entire way of life.

Although most commonly associated with the environment, economic and social issues are also vital to sustainable development.

The UN Division for Sustainable Development promotes the "integration of its economic, environmental, and social components at all levels."

To be sustainable, development must be equitable and protect the social and cultural rights of individuals and communities.

Building a factory may cause GDP to grow, but if it provides unsafe working conditions and low wages, it is not sustainable development.

What are regional trading blocs?

When three or more governments want to make trade with their neighbors easier than with outsiders they can form a regional trading bloc.

To constitute a "bloc," they will agree to lower trade barriers between themselves but maintain common external tariffs against nonmembers.

The most well-known example is the European Union, but they are becoming increasingly prevalent in other regions too.

Mercosur in Latin America, ECOWAS in West Africa, and ASEAN in Asia are three successful examples of regional trading blocs.

But what do these have to do with development? Simple. Think larger markets and economies of scale.

Large markets stimulate production and encourage advanced industries—like steel or chemicals—that wouldn't survive in a small economy.

What are regional development banks?

Developing countries often suffer from a lack of private investment. Regional development banks try to address this deficit.

Important examples include the African Development Bank, the Asian Development Bank, and the Inter-American Development Bank.

These organizations offer medium- and long-term loans for industrial projects in developing countries.

They also assist enterprises with entrepreneurial, managerial, and promotional support.

Originally, multilateral agencies like the World Bank, overseas development agencies like USAID, and national governments provided funds.

As they grew rapidly throughout the 1990s, local and foreign investors came to dominate shareholdings.

The focus on large-scale lending has been criticized as inappropriate for developing countries, where small-scale borrowers predominate.

 # What is debt relief?

Irresponsible lending and borrowing has produced unmanageable debt levels for many developing countries.

Debt relief entails the partial or total forgiveness of debts owed to foreign banks and lending institutions.

Some initiatives, like the joint IMF and World Bank HIPC (Highly Indebted Poor Countries) program, have produced some debt relief.

For many, the debt can be described as being "unpayable," as interest repayments exceed the potential income of a national government.

Even if it is not unpayable, countries have to use vast amounts of public revenue on repayments that could be spent on poverty reduction.

Supporters of debt relief say it is crucial—shifting resources to the domestic economy means governments better serve the people's needs.

But debt relief remains contentious, with some economists and politicians arguing that relief will encourage more irresponsible borrowing.

What is the Gini coefficient?

Ever wondered how we can measure inequality within countries? The Gini coefficient was developed for this very purpose.

It is a mathematical representation of inequality, measured from 0 to 1, with 0 being complete equality and 1 complete inequality.

This standardized value is used to measure inequality in all manner of things, from education to land ownership.

It is most commonly used for income—the real world range is around 0.2 in the most equal countries and 0.7 in the most unequal.

Inequality measurements are important for development —they provide more detail than overall GDP levels.

High levels of inequality are detrimental—they can lead to increases in crime and perpetuate poverty in communities for generations.

What is purchasing power parity?

Measurements of GDP are almost always presented in U.S. $ terms, but $1 in one country can buy a lot more than $1 in another.

Purchasing power parity (PPP) is a calculation that takes this into account when representing GDP in U.S. dollars.

Rather than use simple market exchange rates to represent a GDP expressed in a different currency, PPP produces a standardized measure.

Inflation and the relative cost of living are included to produce a more accurate figure, which is vital to understanding economic growth.

One popular example is *The Economist*'s "Big Mac Index," which uses the price of the popular sandwich to calculate a simplified PPP.

Comparing the price of this standard product in different countries provides a proxy for the relative cost of living.

 # What is microfinance?

In many developing countries, small-scale business predominates. Commercial banks rarely offer them loans, so microfinance fills this gap.

Microfinance institutions directly target the poor and provide small loans (usually less than $500) to those without collateral.

Street vendors, independent traders, and peasant farmers all benefit from these primarily cooperative organizations.

The group lending scheme allows a group to take out a large loan and allocate funds to the individual members who then repay the group.

Credit associations provide interest-free loans. A fixed amount of savings is collected from group members and then redistributed as credit.

The most famous example of microfinance is the Grameen Bank. Founded originally in Bangladesh, it has become a world-renowned institution.

Uncollateralized loans are distributed to groups, who are given business training, with peer pressure ensuring very high repayment rates.

What is foreign direct investment?

Foreign direct investment (FDI) is medium- or long-term investment by an individual or business in a foreign economy.

This mostly takes the form of multinational corporations acquiring or incorporating other businesses or subsidiaries.

Supporters argue it is key to development—it addresses the lack of domestic capital and brings the latest technologies and skills.

Local governments also arguably benefit through increased revenue from taxes on both the higher profits and wages that are created.

Yet to attract FDI, governments have to provide incentives—public subsidies and tax concessions all reduce the potential revenue.

FDI may also stifle domestic entrepreneurship because local firms are driven from the market—corporations are after profits, not development!

What is "hot money"?

Short-term investments in developing countries are often referred to as "hot money"—they can come or go in minutes!

They are held in local stock or currency markets by foreign speculators who move the money around rapidly to profit from small fluctuations.

These financial flows are extremely volatile and their contribution to development is highly contentious.

On the one hand, recipient countries can benefit from the increased availability of capital for local business.

On the other, the volatility of such flows can destabilize an economy and will never be an adequate substitute for long-term investment.

In the mid-1990s, Mexico and Thailand, among others, suffered massive crises as foreign investors pulled out their "hot money."

What use is international aid?

International aid is the transfer of resources from rich to poor countries—it refers to noncommercial, concessional assistance.

Mostly it takes the form of "official development assistance." This comes directly from governments through agencies like USAID.

This aid is intended to help reduce poverty and provide budget support for sectors such as education and health care.

Critics argue that despite the billions spent there have been few positive results. It has made countries worse off and bred corruption.

It is claimed that governments have become dependent, relying on this income rather than encouraging exports or increasing tax revenues.

Yet, although there are problems—particularly related to accountability—the total abolition of international aid is problematic.

Development requires resources that the market alone cannot provide—and aid offers one way for governments to reach those who need them.

What are intellectual property rights?

Intellectual property refers to the ideas, designs, and inventions that constitute a product. A rights regime is designed to protect them.

Copyrights and patents are two of the most common means by which these are defined and enforced.

Supporters of intellectual property rights claim that they are vital for poor countries to grow as they provide an incentive for innovation.

But critics argue that they are mainly beneficial to large corporations and may in fact be harmful to poor countries and their people.

One example is HIV/AIDS—intellectual property rights have long limited the sale of cheaper drugs to poor countries.

Why is China so successful?

The rapid growth and industrialization of China's economy is perhaps one of the most impressive development success stories.

Rapid growth and the increased presence of industry, particularly in the south, have produced a dramatic reduction in poverty.

According to World Bank estimates, in eleven years from 1987 to 1998, those living below the poverty line decreased by nearly 100 million!

Some claim that this success is because of liberalization while others point to the role of government.

On the one hand, the central role of exports in industrialization is often used to support arguments for increased liberalization.

But the effectiveness of industrial policy and prevalence of state-owned enterprises highlights the important role of government.

Unlike in other parts of the world, reforms have been carried out slowly and systematically—there seems little reason for this to change.

 # Why is Argentina not more successful?

Some have referred to the experience of Argentina over the last century as a case of "frustrated development" —but why?

At the turn of the twentieth century, Argentina was among the richest nations—behind only the U.S., Britain, Canada, and Germany.

Its economy thrived as it exported wheat and beef all over the world, primarily to Britain.

After the 1930s, its economy entered terminal decline —British demand dried up and what used to be sent for export was consumed at home.

Efforts to expand industrial production were made in the mid-twentieth century, but instability and external constraints led to failure.

Persistent military coups prevented a coherent economic policy, while multinational corporations limited the space for domestic industry.

Toward the end of the century, liberalization led to trade and fiscal deficits, producing a massive crisis in 2002.

Green economics

Do we need growth? Against all conventional wisdom, green economists argue that we don't. We just need to change our definition of "success." The answer, according to this school of thought, is "steady as she goes."

What is use value?

In classical economics, use value is the amount a buyer is willing to pay or a seller is willing to accept for a commodity.

The use value of a natural resource such as the sea is the price of its fish as food, its shells as jewelry, and its potential for tourism.

The sea has indirect use value in preserving the world's ecosystem and as a habitat for different species.

Green economists believe there are other factors that are more important than use value—known as "nonuse" values.

The sea has existence value in the satisfaction we gain from knowing it exists as a habitat for rare species, even if we never see them.

It has bequest value as it will be around for future generations—which we are willing to pay for even though it doesn't benefit us directly.

Putting a price on the environment enables us to better understand the value of what we might be losing beyond its mere use value.

What is natural capital?

The traditional "means of production" are land, capital, and labor, where the amount of land is fixed and capital is entirely manmade.

Green economists add natural capital to recognize the living element of land that isn't fixed and the element of capital that isn't manmade.

Natural capital is the stock of trees, fish, and minerals that exist in a place and yield a sustainable flow of goods into the economy.

They also provide a place for the economy to operate by creating oxygen, cleansing water, recycling waste, and preventing soil erosion.

Some economists argue that natural capital plays a key role in the economy and provides the "missing link" between GDP and well-being.

Unless we factor it in as a means of production, they claim, we will never have an accurate model of the way the economy really works.

What is throughput?

Throughput is the consumption of natural resources from raw materials through the production process and back into nature as waste.

The greater our consumption, the more there will be of throughput, consumption of finite resources, and waste.

The term was coined by the economist Herman Daly, who was charged with "greening" the World Bank in the 1990s.

He said the opportunity costs (e.g., pollution, resource depletion) of economic growth exceeded its benefits, leading to "negative growth."

His solution was to discourage throughput by taxing the extraction of resources at source, called a "severance tax."

He said we should tax things we want (jobs, income) less, and things we don't want (pollution, depletion) more.

We should focus on quality of throughput rather than quantity—development rather than growth.

What is self-reliance?

Self-reliance is about producing goods and services for which there is local demand, rather than serving the global markets.

It's about generating enough income so that a country or region is not dependent on aid or on employment from global companies.

The model is a national network of "cottage industries," devoted primarily to agriculture, housing, and local infrastructure.

Microcapital helps people improve their income-earning potential by providing finance for education and business start-ups.

Gandhi promoted self-reliance because he thought India was too dependent on the U.K. He wore only local fabrics to support local industry.

Self-reliance goes with plain living and reduced consumption, and places more emphasis on the spiritual standard of life, not just of living.

What is appropriate scale?

Appropriate scale is a concept devised by the German–British philosopher Fritz Schumacher, author of *Small is Beautiful*.

He said the capitalist tendency towards "giantism" was not only unecological but dehumanizing and turned people into slaves of machines.

He suggested that economic growth should be limited to the point of sufficiency and should be based on renewable resources.

Schumacher advocated decentralized production, using affordable technology and locally sourced materials wherever possible.

The starting point for his ideas was Buddhist philosophy, and his approach is also known as Buddhist economics.

In the 1970s, Schumacher advised India's Prime Minister Nehru on rural development and came up with the concept of appropriate technology.

What is entropy?

Entropy comes from the second law of thermodynamics, which says that all energy goes from high to low concentration—from order to disorder.

In keeping with the first law of thermodynamics, energy cannot be destroyed, but it can be transformed and made less accessible.

Sunlight is turned into trees, which turn into coal, which turn into ash; the more inaccessible the energy, the higher its entropy.

Economic activity is a process of turning energy from low entropy (coal, oil) into high entropy (goods, waste). And it's irreversible.

The physical concept was observed in 1824 and applied to economics by Romanian economist Nicholas Georgescu-Roegen in the 1960s.

Green economics is concerned with slowing down this process in order to conserve the planet's stock of high entropy natural resources.

What are alternative measures of GDP?

GDP (Gross Domestic Product) runs counter to the environment. Conservation is regarded as a cost, while cleaning up pollution adds to GDP.

Alternative indices address this issue by including factors such as the cost of natural resources, income distribution, and quality of life.

The Genuine Progress Indicator (GPI) deducts environmental and social cost from economic growth to measure its real, sustainable benefit.

It includes factors such as resource depletion, crime, social breakdown, pollution, and loss of ecosystems.

Applied to Europe and the U.S., the GPI has declined since its peak in 1975, despite a steady rise in GDP.

The Human Development Index measures life expectancy, education, and standard of living, but it doesn't include an environmental factor.

Other indices are the Index of Sustainable Economic Welfare, Gross National Happiness, National Well-Being Accounts, and Happy Planet Index.

What is a steady state economy?

A steady state economy is where GDP neither grows nor contracts, population remains constant, and natural resources are used sustainably.

Unlike classical economics, which assumes constant growth, it assumes growth and natural resources are finite.

Its main principles are: maintain the ecosystem and consume renewables (such as fish and trees) no faster than they can be replenished.

Also, consume nonrenewables (such as coal and oil) no faster than new sources are found; deposit waste no faster than it can be degraded.

The idea of a "stationary state" was first mooted by J. S. Mill in the nineteenth century and was revived by Herman Daly in the 1970s.

 # What is ecological economics?

Ecological economics is a school of thought that asserts that the economy is a sub-category of the planet's eco-system—not vice versa.

It attempts to counter the classical economic view of the environment as an infinitely replaceable commodity of no actual financial value.

Since the environment supplies everything, from raw materials to climate regulation, it must be regarded as a "factor of production."

Some ecological economists want to assign a value to these elements to give them status; others think this turns nature into a commodity.

Ecological economics views society as a metabolism, with a source function (supplying raw materials) and sink function (disposing of waste).

Its purpose is to find the place of human beings within that metabolism, achieving maximum happiness without disturbing the natural balance.

Ecological economics differs from environmental economics in that it's more of a philosophy than a political movement.

Glossary

Absolute advantage
The ability to produce a product more efficiently and therefore more cheaply than one's competitors.

Asset
Something of value owned by a person or firm, e.g., investments, property, or shares.

Bond
A type of security issued by companies and governments to raise capital.

Capital
The machines, buildings, and cash assets that are owned by a company.

Commodity
Any product that can be bought and sold.

Comparative advantage
This is the theory that, even if one country has absolute advantage in all areas of production over another country, it still pays for them to trade. This is because, by concentrating their efforts on the thing they do best, i.e., the area where they have comparative advantage, both countries use their resources most efficiently (see pp. 40, 51).

Consumption
Spending on goods and services by consumers.

Creditor
Person or company giving a loan or buying a bond, i.e., the party to whom credit, or money, is owed.

Debt
Money owed by an individual or firm to another individual or firm, usually a bank.

Debtor
Person or company taking out a loan or issuing a bond, i.e., the party which owes credit, or money.

Default
Failure to comply with the terms of a loan, e.g., paying interest on time.

Deficit
In public spending, when government spends more than it earns in revenue. In balance of trade, when imports exceed exports.

Deflation
A fall in the average price of goods.

Demand
The amount of a good or service that consumers are willing to buy.

Depression
A prolonged fall in economic output, usually measured over two consecutive quarters.

Deregulation
Reducing the red tape that sets controls on business and industry.

Dividends
Share of a company's profit distributed to shareholders.

Economics
The study of how society manages its resources.

Equity
How much a company is worth after deducting all liabilities.

Expansion
A combination of increased investment, greater consumption and high employment.

Externality
An unintended side effect of a certain economic activity, e.g., pollution.

GDP
Gross Domestic Product, used as an indicator of a country's economic performance; usually measured as consumption + investment + public spending + balance of trade (i.e., exports – imports).

Inflation
An increase in the cost of living.

Interest
The amount paid to a lender in return for credit, usually worked out as a percentage per annum.

Investment
The use of money to make more money by buying capital goods or securities.

Labor
The availability of people willing to work, considered one of the three "factors of production," alongside land and capital.

Land
One of the three "factors of production," alongside labor and capital.

Leverage
In finance, the use of financial instruments (i.e., loans) to increase capital. In business, the ratio of debt to equity in a company.

Liberalization
The process of enacting liberal policies, such as privatization and deregulation.

Liquidity
The ease with which an asset can be sold, where cash is at its most "liquid."

Loan
The giving of credit, or money, for a fixed term, usually in return for interest.

Macroeconomics
The study of "big picture" economic factors, such as growth, inflation, and unemployment.

Market
A public place where goods are bought and sold, including stocks and shares.

Merger
When two companies are combined into one, usually brought about through a purchase of shares.

Microeconomics
The study of the inner workings of the economy, such as markets, prices, and buying habits.

Money
A currency (e.g., coins or shells) given in return for services or goods.

Monopoly
When one producer dominates the market for a product or service.

Multilateral
Relating to three or more parties.

Output
The amount of goods or services produced by an individual or firm.

Portfolio
Set of investments owned by an individual or firm.

Privatization
Trransfer of government-owned enterprises into private ownership.

Public good
Something that is consumed by all and impossible not to consume, e.g., air, national defense, and the judiciary.

Recession
A combination of decreased investment, reduced consumption, and high unemployment.

Remittance
Funds transfer from buyer to seller.

Resource
One of the ingredients that make up an economy; usually derived from one of the three "factors of production," land, labor, and capital.

Returns
A business's profit.

Securities
General term for products sold in financial markets, e.g., bonds, shares, options, etc.

Shareholder
The owner of shares in a firm.

Stagflation
A combination of stagnation and inflation, thought impossible until the 1970s' global recession.

Stimulus
The reinvigoration of an economy through government policy.

Subsidy
The partial payment of a good or service, usually by government, to make it viable.

Supply
The amount of a good or service produced by companies.

Surplus
In balance of payments, when exports exceed imports.

Tariffs
A levy imposed by government on a product or service.

Underground economy
Goods and services bought and sold without being declared for tax purposes and therefore not registered as part of GDP; also known as the black market.

Resources

Books

30-Second Economics by Adam Fishwick, Christakis Giorgiou, Katie Huston, and Aurélie Maréchal (Barnes & Noble, 2010)

A Survey of Global Political Economy by Kees van der Pijl (e-book available for free at www.sussex.ac.uk/ir/1-4-7-1 [2009])

Economic Development (9th Edition) by Michael Todaro and Stephen Smith (Pearson, 2006)

E-Z 101 Macroeconomics, 2nd Edition by Jae K. Shim and Joel G. Siegel (Barron's Educational Series, Inc., 2005)

E-Z 101 Microeconomics, 2nd Edition by J. Bruce Lindeman (Barron's Educational Series, Inc., 2002)

Green Economics: An Introduction to Theory, Policy, and Practice by Molly Scott Cato (Earthscan Publications, 2009)

Imperialism: The Highest Stage of Capitalism by V. I. Lenin (International Publishers, 1997 [originally published 1917])

Macroeconomics The Easy Way by George E. Kroon (Barron's Educational Series, Inc., 2007)

My Life and Work by Henry Ford (NuVision Publications, 2007 [originally published 1922])

Naked Economics: Undressing the Dismal Science by Charles Wheelan (W W Norton & Co., 2002)

The Economic Development of Latin America and its Principal Problems by Raul Prebisch (United Nations, 1949)

The Economic Naturalist: Why Economics Explains Almost Everything by Robert H. Frank (Virgin Books, 2008)

The New Economics: A Bigger Picture by David Boyle and Andrew Simms (Earthscan Publications, 2009)

The Undercover Economist by Tim Harford (Oxford University Press, 2006)

Websites

Federal Reserve
www.federalreserve.gov

International Monetary Fund
www.imf.org

Investopedia:
www.investopedia.com

Library of Economics and Liberty
www.econlib.org

The Finance Glossary
www.finance-glossary.com

United Nations Development Programme **www.undp.org**

U.S. Environmental Protection Agency **www.epa.gov**

U.S. Securities and Exchange Commission **www.sec.gov**

Index

Acknowledgments

To Anna, for seeing the funny side.
Nic Compton

To Becky, Lynn, Neil, and Ben—thanks for all your help and support.
Adam Fishwick

Thanks to Sam Knafo, Kees van der Pijl, and Benjamin Selwyn for teaching how things should work, how they do work, and how they could work. Thanks also to Sahil Dutta.
Katie Huston